A Pocketful of Goobers

A Pocketful of Goobers

A Story about George Washington Carver

by Barbara Mitchell
illustrations by Peter E. Hanson

A Carolrhoda Creative Minds Book

Carolrhoda Books, Inc./Minneapolis

For Sara B. Gardner, from the Prof and me

This book is available in two editions:
Library binding by Carolrhoda Books, Inc.,
  a division of Lerner Publishing Group
Soft cover by First Avenue Editions,
  an imprint of Lerner Publishing Group
241 First Avenue North
Minneapolis, MN 55401 U.S.A.

Website address: www.lernerbooks.com

Library of Congress Cataloging-in-Publication Data

Mitchell, Barbara, 1941–
  A pocketful of goobers.
(A Carolrhoda creative minds book)
  Summary: Relates the scientific efforts of George
Washington Carver, especially his production of more than
300 uses for the peanut.
  1. Carver, George Washington, 1864?–1943—Juvenile
literature. 2. Agriculturists—United States—Biography—
Juvenile literature. [1. Carver, George Washington,
1864?–1943. 2. Agriculturists. 3. Afro-Americans—
Biography. 4. Peanuts] I. Hanson, Peter E., ill. II. Title.
III. Series.
S417.C3M58   1986   630'.92'4 [B] [92]   86-2690
ISBN 0-87614-292-7 (lib. bdg. : alk. paper)
ISBN 0-87614-474-1 (pbk. : alk. paper)

Manufactured in the United States of America
  20 21 22 23 24 – MA – 06 05 04 03 02 01

Table of Contents

AUTHOR'S NOTE

Goober is the African word for peanut. It is a very old African word. Goobers kept the slaves alive on their journey from Africa to the West Indies and America's south. Twice a day, the slave traders brought their captives up from the dark hold of the ship onto deck to be fed. The Africans received a cupful of water and then sat ten-to-a-tub for their meal. Sometimes the tub was full of boiled rice. Sometimes it was full of boiled horse beans. More often than not, though, it was full of boiled goobers. Goobers were cheap. The ship's captain had simply to trade an elephant tusk or a bright piece of cloth for many tubs of them when he reached the African shore.

Some of the slaves who ended up in Virginia brought goobers with them and planted them at the sides of their cabins. Because they had grown goobers at home, these little goober patches reminded the slaves of life as it had been in the old country, before the slave traders had come. Goobers were a welcome addition to the fatty bacon and peck of corn the master handed out for food week after week, too. Soon, plantations scattered throughout the South were sporting little goober patches. Then the masters began to plant goober patches, too. The funny-shaped goobers amused their children, they said, and they were good for the hogs.

Most of the old African words are gone, now; gone with the old African stories told around supper fires late into the night. This is a story about a man who lived when peanuts were still called goobers. It's a story about giving and caring. It's a story to remember—every time you have a pocketful of goobers.

Chapter One

George Carver was about a year old when freedom came to the slaves, maybe a bit older. He never knew for sure. Nobody bothered to write down when slave babies were born. Slave babies didn't even have last names. They just took the name of the family that owned them. Their mothers remembered the day they were born, of course. Mothers always remember things like that. But George could not ask his mother about it.

George's mother, Mary, was the only slave Moses and Susan Carver owned. Moses Carver did not believe in owning slaves. But neighbors were few and far between in Missouri during the 1860s, so he had given in and bought Mary to keep Susan company. Susan Carver treated Mary more like a sister than like a slave, folks said. The local Ku Klux Klan did not think much of that. One winter night, they paid a surprise visit to Mary's cabin. Moses Carver scooped up George's older brother, Jim, and ran. Mary stood holding her baby, too terrified to move. The riders in their ghostly costumes took off with the two of them.

Susan Carver was afraid for Mary and her baby. Moses sent out a searcher on horseback to look for them. The searcher came back with Mary's baby. "Some women had it," he said. But Mary was never heard of again. The small rag-wrapped bundle that was George was feverish and coughing. The baby had whooping cough, or maybe something worse. There were no doctors to tell what slave babies had. Their mothers had always just doctored them with herb tea and hoped for the best.

Mary's baby was luckier than most. The Carvers were unusual people. Moses and Susan took George and Jim in to live with them, and Susan nursed the nearly dead baby back to health.

"What was my mother like?" George asked when he grew older.

"Like you, George, quick to learn," Aunt Susan Carver said. "Mary could memorize my quilting patterns faster than butter melting in the sun."

George wanted to go to school. He wanted it more than anything, and he told his plants so every day. The plants were his friends. George had a way with them. There wasn't anything that "Carver's George" couldn't make grow, the neighbors said. There was a school right down the road, and one day George got up the nerve to ask Uncle Moses about it.

"That school is only for white children," Uncle Moses said as gently as he could.

Aunt Susan found an old speller in the attic and taught George his letters, and Uncle Moses taught him his numbers. In the mornings, George took his speller and went down to the schoolhouse. He sat on the doorstep, where he could at least *hear* the lessons. But it wasn't the same as being inside. It just wasn't.

When George was 10, he and Jim walked the 8 miles into town. George came back from Neosho so excited he could hardly talk. "Th-there's a school th-there," he said, "f-for black ch-children." (George stuttered when he got excited.) "I have t-to go to it. I just h-have to, Uncle Moses."

A 10-year-old boy could not walk 8 miles to and from school each day, and the Carvers didn't know anyone in Neosho who could board George. So they persuaded him to wait a couple of years. Maybe then he could strike out on his own. Finally, on a fall morning in 1875, Aunt Susan stood waving 12-year-old George down the road. Wearing a suit cut down from one that had belonged to Moses Carver and carrying a sack of corn dodgers in his hand, George was off to school at last.

He arrived in Neosho tired and hungry, the corn dodgers long gone. Next to the school, he saw a barn. George climbed up into the hay loft and fell fast asleep. In the morning he awakened to see a small black woman in the yard below hanging out laundry. The woman saw George, too.

"Come down here," she ordered.

Mariah Watkins was peppery, but she had a kind heart. She gave George a hearty breakfast and listened to his story. Childless Mariah and Andrew Watkins saw the boy who sat before them as a godsend. They joyfully took him into their home.

School! George loved it. He spent his school-time hours in the crowded shanty that held 74

other students and a teacher. His free time was spent helping Aunt Mariah with the laundry she took in. George loved to read so much that he kept a book propped up in front of the laundry tubs as he scrubbed. Aunt Mariah's Christmas gift to George was a Bible. He was still reading from it when he was 80 years old.

It wasn't long before George had learned all there was to be learned at Lincoln School. The teacher seemed to think that black children could not learn much. George believed he could do anything he put his mind to. He wanted to learn about *everything*, but most especially about plants and how they grew. "Why are geraniums red?" he would ask. "Why do plants grow better in black soil than in yellow soil?" But there was no one to tell him the answers.

"I've got to leave here to find a better school," George said to Aunt Mariah one day.

Aunt Mariah understood. "Our people are hungry for learning, George," she said. "Learn all you can. Then give it all back to them."

Chapter Two

There was a family in town moving to Kansas, and they agreed to take George with them in their wagon. He was about 16 when he arrived in Fort Scott, Kansas, knowing only the people who had given him a ride. Discovering a family that needed a cook, he applied for the job. He had no experience to speak of with cooking and baking, but, as usual, he set about the task believing that he could accomplish it—and he did! It wasn't long before his plump loaves of bread were winning prizes at the county fair.

Whenever George could save the money, he went to school. There were no free books and other school supplies. George had to pay for all of them out of his small salary.

George went from school to school; wherever he could find work. He always looked for a school that was more advanced than the one he had left. In Olathe, Kansas, he was taken in by Christopher and Lucy Seymour, another childless black couple. Aunt Lucy was a laundress, too. She taught George to iron a petticoat so stiff it would stand up by itself. When the Seymours moved to Minneapolis, Kansas, George went with them. There he decided to strike out on his own and set up his own laundry business. He bought a small two-room shack and immediately went to work. The homey, whitewashed building, filled with the flowers George loved, was soon full of friends as well. George was a good storyteller, and he loved to tease his eager audiences. One thing George teased his friends about was his name. There was another George Carver in Minneapolis. The two Georges kept getting one another's mail. George decided to solve the problem by adding a *W* to the middle of his name.

"What does it stand for?" his friends asked.

George thought a moment. "Washington," he said with a wink. And it did, from then on.

"Why do you work and study so hard?" his friends asked.

"Because," George said, "I am going to college, and then I am going south again to help my people."

Attending college was his dream. The day came when it was time to apply. George applied to Highland University, a small school nearby. It was the only one he could afford, and he would have to sell his house to do that. He took the examinations and then began the long wait for the results. George was worried. He was afraid his education had not been good enough, considering all the schools he had attended. He haunted the postman day after day.

The answer came at last. Not only were George's grades good enough, the letter said, but he had won a scholarship!

George walked into the college admissions office full of happiness. He introduced himself. "I am George Carver," he said, "your new student."

The dean looked at him. "But we do not take *Negroes* here," he said brusquely.

That was it. All the hard work, all the outstanding examination grades meant nothing. The hurt went deep down inside George Carver. For the first time in his life, he felt like giving up.

George became truly a wanderer now. One of

the towns he stopped in was Winterset, Iowa, near Des Moines. There he got a job as a chef. One Sunday night he went to visit a local church. George had never cared about denominations. If he saw a church door open, he went in. He stood fascinated this night by the beautiful voice of the choir director. He had always loved to sing, but his infant illness had left his voice thin and weak.

Mrs. Mulholland, the choir director, noticed the lonely looking visitor and invited him home for dinner. It wasn't long before George was taking voice lessons from Mrs. Mulholland in exchange for giving her painting lessons. George was a natural artist, and he loved to paint.

"But you *must* go on to college," Mrs. Mulholland insisted when she had heard about his experience at Highland University.

Mrs. Mulholland was right, he knew. If he was ever going to help his people, he had better get on with the preparation. He applied to Simpson College in Indianola, Iowa, a school sponsored by the Methodist church.

"Welcome to Simpson," the college president said after he had gone over George's excellent records. It was September 9, 1890. George Carver was a college student at last.

The art teacher at Simpson, Miss Budd, took a special interest in George. He showed talent. George discovered that Miss Budd loved plants, too. He asked if he might keep some of his plants in the sunny windows of her classroom. The Simpson art room was soon full of flowers. Miss Budd knew a lot about plants. Her father was the head of the agriculture department at Iowa Agricultural College in Ames, Iowa. "Ames" was America's leading agricultural school. She answered question after question for George. "Flowers get their colors from the foods they are fed," she explained when George asked about this. George experimented with his geraniums. In came a blue geranium for the art teacher.

Secretly, George dreamed of being an artist. One day he told Miss Budd about it. The idea bothered her. Very few artists were able to make a living from their work, and George's talent really went beyond being able to draw. Every leaf, every bloom on his pictures of plants was precisely accurate. The work showed that George knew a great deal about plants. Miss Budd wrote to her father. Then she had a talk with George. He would be able to do more for his people, she felt, as an agricultural scientist than as an artist.

George was disappointed, of course, but the words of Aunt Mariah came back to him: "Learn all you can, George. Then give it all back to our people."

George went to Ames. He proved to be an outstanding student, especially in the field of experimental botany. His professors were soon citing his work in their lectures. By 1896 George Carver was the best-trained black agriculturalist in America. He had earned his masters degree and had been asked to stay on at Ames as a professor. Just over 30, he was one of the youngest teachers on campus.

On April 1 of that year, a letter arrived for Professor Carver from Tuskegee, Alabama. Professor Carver had never heard of Tuskegee, Alabama, but the letter was intriguing. It was from Booker T. Washington, president of Tuskegee Institute. "The Institute trains black students to be teachers, farmers, and technicians," Dr. Washington wrote. He told about the campus. "We have taken over an old plantation. At present, we have one building." He told about the students. "Many come to us barefoot." He told about his dream. "At Tuskegee we aim to teach our students that nothing is beyond them."

Professor Carver walked to the door of his brand-new greenhouse. Spring had just come to the beautiful 900-acre Iowa campus. He had the best land for growing here, the best equipment for experimenting with the crossbreeding of his roomful of rainbow-colored plants. Among his students were the best of America's young agricultural scientists. "Will you come and teach for us?" the letter in his hand asked.

The letter stirred up memories—memories of a small boy sitting on the doorstep of a country school forbidden to him... memories of chopping wood, baking bread, tubs of laundry, oh, the *tubs* of laundry—all to get to school. He also remembered the day he had stood before the dean at Highland University. Professor Carver went over to his desk and wrote out his answer— he would come.

Chapter Three

That October George found himself on a train chugging south to Tuskegee. There were no rolling green hills in Alabama, no fields of rainbow-colored flowers. There wasn't even a shade tree; nothing but a few scrubby pines poking up from sandy soil. What there was, was cotton, cotton, and more cotton. Cotton grew everywhere. It grew right up to the rickety cabins that sat plunk in the middle of it. It was nothing but bumblebee cotton, Professor Carver realized. "Bumblebee cotton" was a nickname for cotton so poor that it was said a bee would not even have to fly to get the nectar from its low-lying blossoms.

Cotton pickers were everywhere—and they didn't look much healthier than the cotton they were picking. Probably have pellagra, Professor Carver thought. The disease was common among poor blacks whose diet was no more than pork, corn meal, and molasses. The people looked tired and sick. The land looked tired and sick. It made George feel sad.

Then there was Tuskegee. Tuskegee was a shock. A student met him at the station with a tired-looking old horse and a rickety surrey. They drove out to the campus. The red and yellow soil all around them was nothing but clay, and it was full of gullies. "Why, an ox could get lost in one of those!" the new professor exclaimed.

The student pointed to a stretch of piney woods. "We call that Big Hungry," he said. The Tuskegee hogs were scrounging there for their supper. They were the skinniest hogs Professor Carver had ever seen.

"And that's our dairy," the student went on. The dairy was a butter churn under a sweetgum tree. There was a tiny blacksmith shop and a string of old slave cabins. "We hold classes in those," the student explained.

Professor Carver soon met Dr. Washington.

The building described in the president's letter was only half finished. "The students are making the brick," Dr. Washington explained. "We expect to be in by spring." He showed the new professor his equipment—one hoe, and Old Betsy. Old Betsy was a blind ox.

The tall young professor with a flower in his lapel leaned down and scooped up a handful of Tuskegee soil. He gave Dr. Washington his gentle smile. "Needs a little fertilizer," he said.

The next day, George met his students—all 13 of them. "Most students come here to get *away* from farming," they told him.

"Come, we are going to take a walk," their new teacher said. The students looked at him. "What for? We came here to learn agriculture."

"You cannot learn agriculture without a lab," Professor Carver answered. He took them around the neighborhood knocking on doors. They came back with old jars, bottles, and other throw-aways. The jars became containers for chemicals. An ink bottle became a Bunsen burner for heating experiments. Bottles were cut down into beakers for pouring. A chipped tea cup and the stub of a drapery rod became a mortar and pestle for grinding and mixing. Tuskegee had a lab.

Not long afterward, Professor Carver took his class for another walk. "Where are we going this time?" the curious walkers asked. Learning was fun with the "Prof."

"To the dump," Professor Carver told them. He led the class up past Big Hungry.

The school dump had sprouted a glorious pumpkin vine. Professor Carver had the students measure it. "It's 37 feet long, Prof!" a student shouted. The gigantic vine was heavy with fat, orange pumpkins.

"You see," Professor Carver said, "there is no finer fertilizer for the soil than the food scraps we throw away." He showed the class how to make a compost pile. "Now you will be able to show the folks back home how to feed their gardens— for free," he added.

By spring the popular new agriculture professor had 76 students. One by one, they hitched themselves up to Old Betsy and plowed Big Hungry and the dump into an experimental farm.

The neighboring farmers watched. "They'll never grow anything on *that* land," they scoffed.

"Where's the cottonseed, Prof?" the students asked when they had spread the fields with the rich black of their compost pile.

"We are going to plant cowpeas," Professor Carver said quietly.

The students looked at him. "Cowpeas!" they said. "You mean we did all this work just to plant cow food?"

The students had taken for granted that they would be planting cotton. *Everybody* back home planted cotton.

"Cowpeas put minerals back into the soil," the professor said. "Cotton has been taking minerals out of this soil for a hundred years."

When the cowpeas were harvested, he invited his students to dinner. The Prof served "meatloaf," "pancakes," and a "potato casserole"—all made from mashed cowpeas. "Now you will have some nutritious new recipes for the folks back home," he said.

The next spring, the students plowed up their cowpea fields. "We're ready for the cottonseed, Prof," they said.

"We are going to plant sweet potatoes," Professor Carver said.

The students looked at him. "Sweet potatoes!" they said. They had had enough of boiled sweet potatoes in their lives. Sweet potatoes were cheap to plant, and they were filling. They had been a staple in poor southerners' diet since slave days.

"For crop rotation," Professor Carver explained. "Our soil needs a rest. And..." he added, "we are going to plant goobers."

"GOOBERS!" the students exclaimed. They had certainly had more than enough boiled goobers in their lives.

"It's an experiment," Professor Carver said.

When the sweet potatoes were harvested, he and his students went to work in the lab. They worked out a hundred new ways to use the sweet potatoes. Sweet potatoes did not *have* to be boiled, the students learned. They could be dried, roasted, and ground. Their sugar and starch content would make a fine laundry starch. They could provide a good quality flour to supplement expensive wheat flour, and they yielded a syrup better than the sorghum that farmers used for making molasses. Professor Carver had the school print shop prepare bulletins on the sweet potato and its uses and distribute them to local farmers. Farmers who could not read were invited to come to the lab and see the results for themselves.

The next spring, Professor Carver's students plowed the sweet potato plants under. "What are we planting this year, Prof?" they asked dubiously.

"Cotton," Professor Carver said.

The students grinned. Cotton at last.

Professor Carver had been working to develop a new cotton to replace Alabama's poor bumblebee cotton. The Tuskegee cotton grew into plump, sturdy bushes, every one just full of fluffy white cotton.

The early 1900s, though, were not good years for cotton of any sort. A hungry little insect known as the boll weevil had begun crawling up from Mexico, chomping cotton all the way. The weevils devoured field after field. The cotton plants just curled up and died. The local farmers came running to Professor Carver. "What can we do! How will we pay our landlords?"

The farmers stood before Professor Carver, waiting expectantly for an answer. The Professor had been out inspecting the Tuskegee goober field. The bright little goober plants were growing away. Weevils didn't care a thing about goobers. Goobers didn't even mind the burning Alabama winds. They just pushed farther down into the soil and waited for the rains to come, then went on growing. "Plow under your sick cotton," Professor Carver said. "Plant goobers."

The farmers laughed. "Goobers!" they said.

"What good are goobers except to munch at the fair?"

"They are good for your soil. They put nitrogen back into it. And they are good for your families, too," Professor Carver said. "Plant goobers."

Chapter Four

Little by little, the farmers began to follow Professor Carver's advice. One crisp October evening, Professor Carver heard a soft tap at his door. It was the widow from a neighboring farm. "I did just as you said," she told the Professor. "I planted my land up in goobers. Now I've put by all I can use in a year and given my hired man the same. Tell me, Professor, what am I to do with the rest?"

Professor Carver made a fast tour around the countryside. Macon County had indeed produced a bumper goober crop. He saw goobers, goobers, and more goobers. They were piled everywhere, right up to the rickety cabins that sat in the middle of them. The awful truth of it all suddenly washed over him. There was not a thing to do with all those goobers.

The Professor went back to his room and shut the door. He pulled up a chair and sat down, sick at heart. "*Why* did you not think this whole thing through!" he asked himself. The Macon County farmers were worse off now than ever before.

At last he got up and went to bed, but sleep would not come. The guilt he felt weighed on him far into the night.

At dawn he went for his daily walk in the woods. He threw himself down on the mossy ground and began to pray. "I had a little talk with my Creator," he said afterward. To Professor Carver, talking to God was as natural as talking to his students. Years later, when he was much in demand as a speaker, he liked to recall how the answer to the perplexing goober problem had come to him in the stillness of the morning. "The Creator gave me a pocketful of goobers," he would say, "and together we went back to the lab and got down to work."

On that morning in October 1915, Professor Carver had gone to the Tuskegee goober patch and then straight to the lab. He locked himself in, put on his flour-sack apron, and shelled the pocketful of goobers. He ground some of the nuts, heated them, and put them under a press. Out came a cupful of oil. The Professor got to work on it.

In what seemed like no time at all, a knock came at the door. It was a worried student. "Your lunch, Prof." Professor Carver had not appeared at either breakfast or lunch.

"Set it down, set it down. Thank you," he said absently. He went on working. The goober oil was wonderful stuff. It blended easily with other substances and was easier to break down than animal fat.

Next he took the dry cake left from the pressed oil. He added a little water and set up an artificial digestion process. By imitating the human digestive system, he would be able to discover the nutritional value of the goober. The little goober cake was packed full of protein, he found. It had more carbohydrate value than potatoes and more vitamins than beef liver.

Professor Carver went back to the remaining

ground-up nuts. Out came a fluid that looked like milk. He added a pinch of salt and a little sugar. He tasted the result. "Well, I declare!" he exclaimed. It *was* milk.

Another knock came at the door. "Your supper, Prof. Prof, are you all right?"

"Yes, yes. Thank you," Professor Carver answered. He ate the supper and the cold lunch and got back to work. He worked on through the night, stopping only to go out to the field for more goobers.

In the morning, he looked at the glass of goober milk. Cream had formed on top. Professor Carver whipped it. Up came a plump pat of butter. He worked on, for a total of two days and two nights, recombining the goober by-products at different temperatures and under different pressures. At last he took off his apron and stepped out into the coolness of a new morning. He was exhausted, but pleased. He had found fats and oils, gums and resins, pectins and proteins. The goober could easily be broken down for use in margarine, cooking oil, rubbing oil, even cosmetics. The milk it yielded was every bit as nutritious as cow's milk, and it took only a handful of goobers to make a glassful. Professor Carver's several days

in the lab had given birth to 20 uses for the goober. His farmers would have no trouble selling their goobers now.

To convince the Macon County businessmen to support the marketing of goobers, he had some of his students prepare a five-course luncheon for them. The lunch was a regular banquet. First came a loaf of crusty bread and bowls of piping hot soup. "Excellent!" the businessmen exclaimed. On came the salad—a big bowl of "Carver's greens." Then the entrée—baked chicken loaf and a rich creamed vegetable. "Zesty!" the businessmen said. The students brought on the dessert—ice cream and cookies.

When the delighted guests had settled back for coffee and a piece of candy, Professor Carver stood up. "Gentlemen," he said, "I want you to know that everything you have enjoyed for lunch this afternoon (excepting the greens, of course) has been prepared from goobers."

The businessmen had a hearty laugh. "All right, all right," they said, "you have our full support."

Goobers grew into a new industry in the South. A group of goober growers joined together to form the United Peanut Association of America. (It was 1919 and they preferred to use the "modern" term for goober.) Their president invited Professor Carver to speak at the organization's first annual meeting the next fall. Some of the members did not think much of having a black man as guest speaker, but their chief officer insisted. The Tuskegee professor knew more than any man alive about peanuts, he felt.

Professor Carver packed two wooden boxes of specimen bottles and took the train to Montgomery for the meeting. He went to the Exchange Hotel and asked to be taken to the room where the Peanut Association was gathering. "The peanut men have gone over to City Hall," the doorman said.

Professor Carver picked up his heavy boxes and walked down to City Hall. "The peanut men were here, but they have gone to the hotel," he was told.

Professor Carver lugged his boxes back to the hotel. The doorman looked significantly at a sign above his head—NO COLORED.

The peanut men—all of them white—had been there all the time. Their guest was being given the run-around.

"My name is Carver. I am expected," Professor Carver said quietly.

The doorman made no response.

"Perhaps you will take the president of the association a note," Professor Carver suggested.

The note was delivered. A bellhop soon appeared. He took Professor Carver around to a back door and up a back elevator to the meeting room. "My farmers needed me to speak for them. And my Creator helped me to remember that this was no time to go off in a huff over hurt feelings," George said afterward.

It was two o'clock by the time he was ushered into the hot, stuffy meeting room. Professor Carver was warm and tired, but he did not let it show. He simply began lining up his peanut specimens, making jokes as he worked. The little parade of bottles glimmered in the afternoon sun. The peanut men watched closely.

Professor Carver held up the 31 bottles one by one. The men stared wide-eyed at milk drinks, cheese, ice cream, pickles, shoe polish, stains and dyes, and linoleum—all made with by-products of the peanut.

The congressman from Alabama stood up. "I propose we invite Professor Carver to represent us before Congress at the upcoming hearing on import duties," he said.

Cheers went up from the Peanut Association. Their president gave a sigh of relief. The Tuskegee professor had won the men's hearts. Besides, they needed all the help they could get to convince Congress to raise import duties on peanuts. A new import duty would help southern farmers tremendously. The importation of peanuts from the Orient would soon put them out of business if the low rate of $\frac{3}{8}$¢ per bushel was allowed to continue.

Chapter Five

A telegram soon arrived at Tuskegee from Washington, D.C. "Expecting you January 20, 1921." No sooner had the invitation become known on campus, than the ladies of the faculty began to nag the Professor about what he would wear. "Surely you're not going to wear *that* suit," they said.

"That" suit was the only suit Professor Carver owned. It had been a Christmas gift from his fellow students at Ames. Professor Carver rarely wore it. He liked to work in a comfortable old gray sweater and baggy work pants.

"If a suit is what the congressmen want to see, I can send them one in a box," he said mildly.

"But surely you'll not wear one of *those* ties," the ladies insisted. Professor Carver loved long, flowing ties. He wove them himself from natural fibers and dyed them startling colors with natural dyes. He was likely to appear in pokeberry purple, oak-leaf green, or broomstraw orange.

In January he boarded the train for Washington wearing his 28-year-old Ames suit and his favorite corn-husk yellow tie.

At the Washington station, he found a porter and asked to have his specimen cases transported to the House of Representatives. "Sorry, Grand-pop," the porter said. "I'm to meet some professor from Alabama and take him to that very place." Professor Carver hailed a cab for his specimen cases.

When Professor Carver arrived at the House of Representatives, the peanut men greeted him with unhappy news. The subject of peanuts was not likely to be brought before the congressmen any time soon. "I'll be back later," Professor Carver told them, and off he went to the Washington Zoo.

The subject of peanuts had still not come up by noon the next day, and the peanut producers were worried. The congressmen were tiring. At four o'clock, the clerk finally called for the first peanut spokesman. The weary congressmen barely listened to him. "Are there any other witnesses on behalf of higher import duties on the peanut?" the chairman asked sleepily.

The clerk read off Professor Carver's name. Professor Carver started down the aisle with his two heavy boxes. The room got suddenly quiet. A loud remark cut through the silence. "Reckon he's a right happy nigger when he has a water-melon to go with his peanuts."

There could be no doubt that the man now standing before them had heard the comment. Professor Carver went about lining up his exhibit on the clerk's desk. The chairman spoke. "Due to the lateness of the hour, our present speaker will have 10 minutes in which to present his case."

Ten minutes! Why it will take that long to wake up this sleepy group, Professor Carver thought. He held up his first specimen bottle, explaining that it contained soil conditioner made from peanut hulls. The silent room echoed with the sound of snickering. The congressman from Texas jumped up. "Here, here. Let's have order. This man knows a great deal about his subject."

The room grew still again. "What does he know about import duties?" a congressman called out.

Professor Carver answered for himself. "Not a thing. I came here to talk about peanuts."

The congressmen chuckled. Professor Carver popped a crunchy combination of sweet potatoes and peanuts into his mouth. He chewed with obvious enjoyment. "I am sorry you gentlemen cannot taste this delightful breakfast food," he said sadly. "I will just have to taste it for you." George heard more chuckles.

Professor Carver went on quickly. He had his audience with him now. He held up flour, milk, cheese, instant coffee, cooking oil, peanut butter, and pickles. The congressmen leaned forward in their chairs. "Can you get chocolate?" one of them asked seriously.

Professor Carver smiled, "Certainly," he said. He held up a powder for flavoring ice cream. "The peanut is one of the most nutritious foods in the world," he went on. "I could show you dozens of uses." He looked over at the clerk. "But of course my 10 minutes are up."

"This is very interesting," the chairman said. "Go on, please. You have as much time as you want."

Professor Carver did go on, for another hour. He showed food for farm stock, face cream, shaving lotion, ink, shoe polish, dyes, and more. At the end of the presentation, the congressmen all stood up and applauded loudly. "Come back again," they called. "And bring more of your products with you." They voted for a 4¢ per bushel import duty on peanuts.

Newspapers all over the country carried the story. Suddenly the professor from Tuskegee was famous. Letters poured into the Tuskegee town post office in such a great heap that a special branch had to be set up at the Institute. Invitations to speak came from farm groups, civic groups, schools, and churches. Job offers came from famous inventors like Thomas Edison and Henry Ford.

Professor Carver accepted the speaking engagements but turned down all the job offers. "My work is here with Dr. Washington," he said. He did go to Detroit to take part in a convention of scientists, farmers, and industrialists on chemurgy—the new science that studied how to put farm wastes to use. He and Henry Ford became great friends. From then on, Henry's private railroad car was often pulled up at the

Tuskegee station. A room was set aside at Michigan's Dearborn Inn for Professor Carver's use whenever he could get away from his work at Tuskegee.

The state of Alabama sent a peanut exhibit to the New York World's Fair in 1925. It took first prize. The college at Ames and the University of Rochester in New York gave Professor Carver honorary doctorate degrees. "All of those things are very fine," he said. But none of the honors meant as much to him as his daily work with his students and the local farmers. "I learn from them," he said.

On weekends he and a student named Tom Campbell loaded up a wagon with a cream separator, a purebred hog, a fine specimen of a cow, and prize Tuskegee vegetables. Carver called it his moveable school. He and Tom went all over the countryside with it, showing the farmers the latest developments in agriculture. They taught the farmers' wives how to can and dry fruits and vegetables, and how to weave and make other crafts to brighten their cabins, which were now stained attractive colors developed in the Tuskegee lab.

The Prof's door stood open to anyone, black

or white, who sought his help. He especially loved to have the children come to him. He taught a class for them, took care of their sick pets, and took them on walks to explore the Alabama countryside. They were invited into his lab to look at the windows full of plants, the glass cases that held his collections, and the mysterious bottles that held his experiments. He told them stories around the old stove that still heated his chemicals, even though the Tuskegee lab had long since been modernized.

Professor Carver never had children of his own. He never married. "What wife would put up with a husband who gets up at four in the morning to look at plants?" he asked. But each and every one of his students was his child. Long after they left Tuskegee, his students kept in touch with him.

Tom Campbell and his family often invited Professor Carver to spend Thanksgiving and Christmas with them. The Prof always arrived early, with a pocketful of goobers for the children.

MORE ABOUT
GEORGE WASHINGTON CARVER

1. Historians have placed Carver's birthdate about 1864, though some say it may have been as early as 1861.

2. Miss Budd and Carver's classmates at Simpson sent him a bouquet of red carnations for his graduation from Ames. He stuck one in his buttonhole and wore a fresh flower there every day of his life from then on.

3. Professor Carver's students affectionately called him the "Prof." To the local farmers and their families, he was known as the "Professor."

4. Professor Carver found that his students knew little about the value of green vegetables in the diet. He introduced them to the many edible greens that grew wild around Tuskegee. They jokingly called them "Carver's greens" whenever they appeared in the college dining hall.

5. Professor Carver was often the victim of racial prejudice, to which he always responded with grace. In 1923 he received the NAACP's (National Association for the Advancement of Colored People) Spingarn Medal, both for his contributions to science and for his contribution to better understanding between the black and white races.

6. Professor Carver donated his life's savings to the Carver Foundation at Tuskegee, which gave scholarships to needy students so that they might have the opportunity to learn. He also personally supervised the placement of exhibits showing his life's work in the Carver Museum, first established in the Tuskegee laundry room.

7. Henry Ford had a replica of Carver's mother's cabin built at Greenfield Village in Dearborn, Michigan; the sight of it moved Carver to tears.

8. George Washington Carver died on January 5, 1943. He had by that time discovered over 300 uses for the goober.